Printed in the United States of America

First Printing, 2017

ISBN 978-0-9974597-3-9

Stone Road Publishing
Chicago, IL 60618

# FREE RANGE BRANDS

## Join the New Breed of Agile Brands

NICOLE ERTAS

FREE RANGE BRANDS

To tease out what's true,
what matters and what works;
To enjoy the filtered and unfiltered,
wherever it's found - -

I dedicate this work to my parents,
Helga and Alexander Ertas,
and to my beloved son,
Colton.

FREE RANGE
BRANDS

FREE RANGE

BRANDS

# CONTENTS



FREE RANGE BRANDS

# WE ARE HERE

We have been for awhile.
But maybe you haven't noticed.
Which isn't a surprise.

Because very few brands have.
And that's why we're disengaging from them.
But those who have noticed, have our hearts. Our imaginations.
Our energy and our attention.

So you can keep talking if you want.
But you're talking to yourself.

You can pretend it's because we don't love brands. But that's not true.
They're a huge part of our lives. They can be liberating and satisfying.
Expressive, adventurous, influential, informative, or connective.
A single brand can be more powerful than a world leader.

But guess who's in charge?
We are.

We are now driving the conversation.
We are rewriting the rules.
We use our brands to do better. To be better.
Not just to have better.

We are **not** your consumers.

We are **Lords, Lovers, Hackers, and Hawks**.

And we'd like you to get to know us.

FREE RANGE BRANDS

# I

# FREE RANGE BRANDING

# FIRE,
# FLIGHT,
# AND THE RISE OF
# THE FREE RANGE BRAND

FREE RANGE
BRANDS

WELCOME TO

# NOWHERE

*hello!*

Every year, in the last week of August, the countdown clock hits Zero. The gates open, and over 70,000 people of all demographics, cultures, and levels of socio-economic status slowly roll down the once-desolate, single-lane road, past the "Welcome to Nowhere" sign.

From all over the world, they come to spend a week together in a nearly unlivable environment, where the temperature swings from winter-like conditions to the blinding heat of a dry desert within a day. 70mph winds and throttling dust storms paralyze, severe dehydration is a very real risk, and entry past the gates requires you accept the possibility of Death. Yet they come. And every year, more and more join them.

The organizers of Burning Man don't pretend to know what each new year will bring. They set up the structures, define the principles, and when the gates open, the community creates the magic.

In one week, Black Rock City transforms the desert outside a ghost town into the third-largest city in Nevada. Out from the dry dust emerges a powerfully connected and passionate community, not built by its leaders, but emblazoned and self-regulated by those who show up.

* * *

*December 10, 2012*

In Capetown, South Africa, eager contestants attempt to take flight in DIY deathtraps. Rules require power to be strictly limited to human muscle, gravity, and imagination, and the craft to be constructed entirely of environmentally friendly materials. On this day, a record 220,000 people cheer as each contending team or individual takes a seconds-long, flying nose-dive right into the sea.

Over 135 Red Bull Flugtag events have crowned winners around the world, from John's Mighty Flying Gazpacho in Auckland New Zealand, to a catapulted pilot named Stonebird in Croatia, to The Flying Turkeys in Istanbul. The current reigning champions are The Chicken Whisperers from Long Beach, CA with a record flight of 258 feet in front of over 100,000 fans. For 20 years, communities have flocked to witness and fuel the competition of handmade, human-powered flying contraptions launched off a seaside pier. Red Bull's Flugtag event has become a cultural pilgrimage for many, which is literally and figuratively powered by the brand that "gives you wings."

In 1991, Red Bull was the first energy drink on the market in the US. The product itself was disruptive and the consumer need for energy was palpable. Any respectable marketer would have launched this new product by positioning it as a revolutionary new way to energize, in a breakthrough drink form, made with an exotic, powerful and proven ingredient called Taurine. Problem/Solution. And in two years, it would have been one of many, traveling through the brand lifecycle from innovative, to mature, to its grave in a saturated marketplace, trying to reclaim its cache as "the first," but left behind as its once-loyal followers became star struck with fresh new brands that captured their attention. And the cycle would begin again.

But today's emerging stars don't wallow in the shallow confines of material thinking. They live and die by principles and values, not flavors, forms, and ingredient claims.

Many energy drinks have since come and gone, some still linger, and more will come. They'll boast about their energy-giving powers, exotic ingredients, great flavors, better prices, and cool packaging.

Meanwhile, Red Bull barely innovates on product form or flavor, yet the franchise remains the best-selling energy drink in the world, at nearly six billion cans a year and growing.

The "Red Bulls" of brands were the disrupters—the outliers. Marketers saw their achievements as remarkable and worthy of contemplation, but one of the few special ones—not like something everyone could do.

Since the 50s, the large, legacy brands controlled the global marketing channels and media. Without the deep pockets to get on TV to build awareness or pay for distribution to get in a consumer's hands, nearly all no-name challenger brands lived on the fringe, locked behind barriers that were rarely surmountable.

The legacy brands solidified their marketplace foothold by establishing processes of control. Global brand models are rooted in controlling the product, the channels, the message, the voice, the experience, and the interaction. Learning, innovation, evolution, and market dominance are all orchestrated through proven models of controlled iteration, testing, and execution plans.

But in the short span of the past few years, these test-validated brands have suddenly found themselves in an open, unpredictable arena, where very few rules now govern how a brand is positioned, where it is placed, and how it is talked about. And, now, for the first time, the innovative, no-name brands that were once too small to be any real threat are becoming anything but. They're showing up on shelves that were once unavailable to any brand without big bucks for TV support and slotting fees. They're gaining traction an[illegible]it-ing a following faster than the old-school brands can [illegible] validate a self-identity.

And consumers, once passively grateful for w[illegible]

don't be

The leader of

# THE IRRELEVANT

FREE RANGE BRANDS

and delighted to be offered a new flavor or color of the same old thing every couple years, are reorganizing themselves, hijacking brands, and taking over the airwaves. They're tearing down the veils of marketing and forcing companies to open the kimono.

This isn't just a digital revolution. This is total brand anarchy. The landscape that was once dominated by the giants has now totally up-ended. There are no proven strategies to win. Any tactic that won yesterday is now obsolete—not for use again. And all that is certain is that this new, ever-changing landscape demands a level of fluidity and flexibility that has not been seen before.

The brand leaders who still spend their days orbiting around epic annual plans, strategizing, analyzing, re-planning, and endlessly testing are sure to be the future leaders of The Irrelevant.

These brands, tethered to their old models of control, will undoubtedly struggle to find their footing in today's world. But the brands that can learn how to set themselves up to let go will thrive in today's unpredictability and navigate with fluidity. They will soar.

These are the Free Range Brands.

# WHAT IS A
# FREE RANGE BRAND?

FREE RANGE
BRANDS

THE KING IS
DEAD
FREE RANGE
BRANDS

Many of the dynasty brands are hitting their wall and beginning a slow march to death. They are applying old, static rules in the dynamic, Free Range arena. These brands are tightly tethered to old models of learning, decision-making, and consumer interaction. By today's new standards, they are slow to innovate and unable to engage, and have a lack of conviction, an addiction to testing, and an astounding inability to get off the Habitrail.

These brands are relying on scale and their dominance of the dying supermarket channel. But like a high-speed photocopier slowly running out of ink with each new copy it makes, so too will the broadcast brands slowly lose their meaning as repeated, one-way, brand-centered messages get washed out in today's high-engagement arena.

Unlike the tethered nature of traditional brands, Free Range Brands are untethered. Both Free Range Brands and Tethered Brands may seem similar at first blush. Both can launch provocative creative that gets temporary engagement. Both can support philanthropic efforts to show they have purpose.

But rather than engaging consumers with a pre-programmed call to action, Free Range Brands unleash a call to the wild, teeing up ideas or throwing down the gauntlet to inspire and ignite stampedes. Free Range Brands manifest cultural momentum. As a result, they thrive in ways never imagined or pre-defined by the brand team.

# CAGE MATCH

| TETHERED BRANDS | vs. | FREE RANGE BRANDS |
| --- | --- | --- |
| RIGID | | AGILE |
| PRESCRIBED | | TRANSCENDENT |
| CONSPICUOUS | | STEALTH |
| ORCHESTRATED | | RECEPTIVE |
| SOVEREIGN | | COMMUNAL |
| DEFENSIVE | | ADAPTABLE |
| TESTED | | INSTINCTUAL |

FREE RANGE BRANDS

# HOW TO SPOT A FREE RANGE BRAND

Free Range Brands can be spotted by seven distinct behaviors that set themselves apart from their tethered counterparts.

1. They are agile. They are adept at reinventing themselves and quickly responding to unpredictable situations;
2. They forge emotional bonds with their consumers by laddering up functional positionings to transcendent platforms;
3. They appeal to large cohorts in a rather covert manner, rather than the conspicuous approach preferred by traditional brands;
4. Their approach to learning and evolution is often less orchestrated and more receptive to unexpected insights;
5. They activate a community-based, bottom-up expansion, compared to a traditional top-down, corporate push;
6. They are comfortable adapting in the face of adversity versus defending pre-determined decisions;
7. And lastly, they make decisions quickly, almost instinctually, versus relying on testing and validation.

1

FREE RANGE BRANDS

ARE

# AGILE

Urban Outfitters didn't rest on its past success model or brand equity when Amazon moved into the fashion business.

Rather than rooting its heels in its current way of thinking, Urban Outfitters made a strategic pivot, reframing the corporate proposition of offline versus online. "We are no longer a $3 billion company with 20%+ penetration of e-commerce. We are a $600 million e-commerce company that has 500 highly differentiated, productive stores in great locations around the world," said Matthew Kaness, former Chief Strategy Officer of Urban Outfitters. The company reengineered its practices to be consistent with an e-commerce company, while leveraging its store assets as retail showrooms that sell the culture.

Similarly, Best Buy also stared down the Amazon threat by refocusing on core assets that set it apart from Amazon: brick and mortar stores, service, and delivery. Best Buy redesigned over 1,400 stores to elevate the interactive experience with products and people, built a state-of-the-art interactive Manhattan showroom, leveraged the Geek Squad service team to make over 4 million house calls a year, and actually beat Amazon on delivery by using its store locations as distribution centers, cutting delivery speed down to under two days.

Contrast that with Blackberry, Kodak and MySpace, all huge brands that dominated their categories not that long ago. But when the market evolved, these organizations had one choice: change or die.

You know the end of these stories.

# 2

## FREE RANGE BRANDS ARE

# TRANSCENDENT

Free Range Brands are highly adept at elevating their perspective to take in a greater view. They set their sights in the distance, reaching for a higher plane. Functionality is material; Free Range Brands align with the immaterial. Solving for deficiencies has a shelf life; reaching for ideals allows for fluidity, reinvention, and freedom.

Over 20 years ago, Kate Spade tapped into a whitespace in handbag fashion that sat between high-end bling and functional drab: Simple Elegance. The team elevated the brand to embrace the platform of "Graciousness." The platform of Graciousness then informed every brand decision going forward, such as store location and merchandising, leading to the idea of selling flowers in stores to bring the brand platform to life. Even non-Kate Spade merchandise was added to complete the overall brand experience of Graciousness.

Graciousness, untethered from "fashion," weathers time and trends, and transcends generations with ease. As a result, Kate Spade is a global powerhouse worth over $1 billion in sales, largely due to the management team's commitment to brand consistency.

Whole Foods could have been just a better health food store. At the time, health food stores traditionally embodied some sort of sacrifice, be it taste or texture. But rather than positioning to offer superior-tasting health food, Whole Foods laddered way up to make a bold move and grab healthy indulgence, extending health from "body" health into mind and spirit health, influencing an entirely new way of thinking about the food we eat and the world we want to create. This higher plane opened up a broad opportunity to bring in dimension, reinvention, and human connection, far beyond functional food labels.

# 3

## FREE RANGE BRANDS ARE

# STEALTH

Free Range Brands don't often seize their prey by pounding their chests and proclaiming power. They come from behind. They're more savvy and stealth.

BUZZBALLZ—small, tennis-ball sized, pop-top cans of pre-mixed cocktails—quietly rolled into Millennials' summer beer coolers by going rampant under the radar on Instagram. BUZZBALLZ' distinct size, shape, and fun names and claims (Floatable, Non-Explodable) made them an Instagram hit, largely going unnoticed by the big brands.

When Eat24 wanted to compete against established GrubHub, it faced a daunting battle—GrubHub, had $84 million in venture financing, while Eat24 had $0.

So, they found the back door to the main stage. Seeking to stretch every penny, the team uncovered a high-traffic, relevant advertising opportunity with zero competitive clutter: online porn. Identifying a perfect opportunity to gain ad impressions that cost 90 percent less than Google, Twitter, or Facebook made porn the perfect media channel for the bold company to give millions of customers a chance to keep their pants off and order-in. The result? They quickly expanded to over 750 cities nationwide and were swiftly acquired by Yelp.

The Super Bowl might have been the place to be when a brand had the funds for the big leagues. But today, Free Range Brands know there is great value in laying low.

FREE RANGE BRANDS

ARE

# RECEPTIVE

Free Range Brands learn with open minds and resist pre-determined expectations. Learning isn't limited to controlled, screened, and moderated research. That's reserved for the Tethered Brands that feel safer in a cage.

Free Range learning seems to be more open, evolving, and iterative. Free Range Brands welcome and integrate insights in real time from unexpected places. Free Range learning happens beyond the confines of orchestrated focus groups and quantitative research.

As young enthusiasts of the 70-year-old LEGO brand aged, adult communities of LEGO fans emerged and connected with each other online to share ideas, buy and sell pieces, and inspire each other with images of their unique LEGO creations. For years, LEGO saw this offshoot of adult fans as "weird," and continued to focus its research and insights on its core target, children.

Forced into a strategic shift by a decade of declines, the LEGO team opened its mind to engaging with this rogue and off-target fan base. The brand instantly struck marketing gold. Not only did this group become a viable new market for innovation, they were rich with insights and ideas that have taken the brand from a seemingly irretrievable slide into what is now referred to as "The Apple of Toys."

LEGO has since catapulted this adult community to a leading source of new product ideas and feedback on innovation in development.

For example, adult, male LEGO enthusiasts in their 40s and 50s who were collaborating on technical LEGO projects are now credited with connecting the brand to a market of male, teenage robot enthusiasts. They provided insights to the brand team on hardware, software, design, and usability, expanding LEGO's knowledge and capabilities far outside the capacity of internal R&D. In fact, one avid fan and technical expert, John Barnes, helped LEGO expand and produce robotic sensors that revolutionized LEGO Mindstorms to include infrared receiver sensors, sensor multiplexes, barometric sensors, and touch sensors.

Chicago architect and adult LEGO enthusiast Adam Reed Tucker was behind LEGO breaking into an entirely new global distribution channel of museums, souvenir shops, and bookstores. His concept was "to capture the essence of a particular landmark into its pure sculptural form ... in a small scale." Architectural kits include the Empire State Building, the White House, the Brandenburg Gate, and Frank Lloyd Wright's landmark Fallingwater residence in Pennsylvania.

Free Range learning isn't limited to external sources. Turning inward has profound benefits. Studies at MIT are showing that the more people within an organization engage with each other (both within their teams and throughout the internal organization), the more the overall creative output surpasses the collective intelligence of individual members.[†] The sum is greater than the parts. It's the connections that change the game.

Whether it's roaming internally, scavenging online, or just exploring without business purpose, Free Range Brands know that big ideas live where we may never expect to find them.

Giddy up.

† Professor A. S. Pentland, MIT, 2015

"If you stop going to fairs, concerts and bars, and you're just working, you lose touch with all that. You have to refill the reservoir."

-Airbnb CEO Brian Chesney

# 5

## FREE RANGE BRANDS ARE

# COMMUNAL

Tethered Brands are used to controlling the boundaries of play from atop a monarch's throne. But these brands are quickly losing relevance, as modern brand building is no longer a top-down, one-way effort.

A Free Range Brand moves beyond the traditional social media platforms and creates its own communities. It can be done by connecting to and fueling shared interests, such as Sephora's Beauty Talk and Amex's Open Forum for small business owners. It can evolve from long-running promotions such as Doritos' Crash the Super Bowl submissions and viewers. Or even through crowd-sourcing, crowd-funding and idea-sourcing, such as Threadless, the t-shirt empire built entirely by user-submitted designs.

The "sharing economy" demonstrates the profound shift to community-built brands. Uber, Lyft, Waze, Airbnb ... all huge brands that exploded onto the scene based on the philosophy of community sourcing of property and information.

Free Range Brands know that they need to embrace this new world by letting consumers in it, rather than continuing to control it.

Brand viability can no longer be conceptualized and executed solely by the brand teams; it must be released to be manifested by the brand community. We can build the structures, but it is the brand community that gives the brand life.

Frosty needs his hat.

6

FREE RANGE BRANDS

ARE

# ADAPTABLE

All brands sometimes find themselves on the wrong side of the electric fence. The difference is that Free Range Brands can clearly see the situation for what it is and use the opportunity to apologize, course correct, and reinforce their beliefs through swift actions. The end result garners consumer respect on an entirely new level.

McDonald's has faced endless attacks for its low wages, defending its position by offering absurd sample budgets for low-income wage earners. The CEO's flippant remarks just fueled the flames. Rather than finding a way to connect and engage, McDonalds just left a rancid taste in the mouths of customers, employees, and the public at large, inspiring late-night comic rants and rattling watchdog communities.

Weeks after she was named GM CEO, Mary Barra was faced with the 2014 ignition switch crisis. Her public response? Point the finger at "Old GM," distancing herself from owning any responsibility of the issue. The issue quickly escalated as she found herself ridiculed by the Senate, and in the opening sketch of Saturday Night Live.

Contrast these bad responses with Jet Blue having left over 130,000 passengers stranded on Valentine's Day. The company was publicly vilified. But with a swift, honest, and humble response, coupled with highly visible, proactive, and immediate action plans, Jet Blue instantly regained and even elevated the respect of its customers and the traveling community.

7

FREE RANGE BRANDS

ARE

# INSTINCTUAL

Free Range Brands know that today's biggest opportunities don't come in a pitch from an agency partner anymore. They present themselves in unknown places and disappear quickly. Free Range Brands understand that it's critical to know when to engage and when to take a pass. They don't wait to test and validate every opportunity.

When Kit Kat jumped into the Free Range by branding the new Android phone, it didn't take the traditional path of validating such a bold move, especially since chocolate and technology are completely unrelated.

Nestle's chief marketer didn't waver on the decision when it presented itself; the deal was rumored to have been accepted within an hour for no remuneration. "You can go round the swimming pool 10 times wondering if the water is cold or hot or you say: 'Let's jump.'"

Instinct is one of a Free Range Brand's greatest weapons against an established competitor, as most large brands lumber through layers of internal approvals and consumer validation for every move.

# Adapt or Die

Traditional brand leaders have been groomed and pedigreed to operate off decades of best-in-class thinking proven to model consumer behavior to stimulate trial, purchase, and loyalty. They analyze, test, and build all the insights and learnings into epic strategy plans. Innovation processes are fail-safe with well-oiled testing regimens. Internal checks and balances are rigidly in place to ensure top-to-bottom and cross-functional alignment with single-point accountability back to brand owners. The big brands are run by the best and the brightest.

The system is tight, well built, and a proven model for success.

Until now.

Despite the most intelligent and innovative efforts to leverage and engage in the new age of marketing, the models that were once proven success engines for brand building are now relics of the pre-digital world. All were built to optimize a linear, controlled system that flowed forward, emanating from a brand monarch. Today's brand evolution flows forward, backward, circular, sideways, and parallel all at once. Staying true to the old models is just operating on old hardware.

It is often far easier to hide behind the elephant in the boardroom, celebrating a temporary, quarter-point bump in market share from some short-term, lackluster line extension than it is to take real chances—the ones that change businesses.

The world our brands live in has permanently changed. Brand Managers are not the brand owners anymore. The king is dead. Trying to lead from the throne is holding onto the power of an era gone by, and will only bring a brand empire down faster.

# WHAT KIND OF BRAND DO YOU HAVE?

*PRODUCT, POSER OR PLATFORM?*

# Product, Poser or Platform?

An unshakable brand positioning, defined and validated by consumer testing, generally lies at the foundation of many of the world's biggest brands. Unfortunately, traditional positioning is a model that simply doesn't serve a brand well anymore; it is purposely structured to be tightly tethered to static communication, which doesn't allow for fresh, spontaneous consumer engagement.

Unlike the tethered positioning of traditional brands, Free Range Brands are untethered. They do not seek to position themselves on an unmet or functional need, but rather on a platform for communities to engage.

Brands today can fall into one of three categories: A brand can be a Product, a Poser, or a Platform.

FREE RANGE
BRANDS

# 1. Be a Product

Most products or services evolved from fulfilling a marketplace need, which is generally, at its core, a functional offering.

The biggest global brands in the world have been built on a foundation of a deeply rooted, product-marketing model. It was a powerful model in the pre-digital age because the marketplace was dominated by a handful of brands that could generally differentiate themselves from each other by their functional offerings. The basic positioning statement, clearly articulating brand points of difference, became the foundation to clearly segment functional offerings for discreet demographic audiences.

In a fairly controllable, structured environment, a brand could carve out its niche, protect its base and methodically line extend or jump into premium or discount territories. And since barriers to entry were prohibitive for smaller brands, competition remained limited, allowing enough elbow room for brands to each have a fairly distinct market space.

Tethered Positioning roots the brand in a functional story; articulating and filling the unmet need to conclude the story. The story is uninspiring; there is no Part II, let alone a daily reinvention that leaves brand enthusiasts engaged. The brand is set up for commoditization, monotony and consumer disinterest. As the brand tries to participate in the modern world of social engagement, it often finds it really has nothing much to say. It can mainly talk about itself in ways that are generally self-focused and uninteresting to the listener. It is confining, static, and soulless. It has a very short shelf life.

Tethered Brands often emerge from a problem-solution story, and then tend to become constrained in innovation. When the competition addresses that same problem with a product or price that is equal or better (and it will), the only linear next step is to find another unmet consumer need that fits with the brand's original functional offering, aka, the line extension. Same problem, same solution ... different flavor, different color. And when innovation was only expected every few years, there was time to optimize, test, and validate the most compelling new product for a target demographic.

But we know this era has passed. Yet, most of these brands have not evolved and are struggling to figure out why they've lost their market position.

To be "relevant," brands must show up across social channels and entertain, converse, and engage. They must reinvent, not just in form, but in word and deed. Not surprisingly, many are finding themselves tongue-tied on Twitter, struggling for something to talk about to engage their audiences.

Traditionally positioned products struggle to be relevant to today's consumer.

# 2. Be a Poser

As brand empires grew, so did the need to protect their base and seek new areas for expansion. Functional differentiation was no longer enough. Brands went deep with consumers to tap into consumer insights, emotional needs, and relevant consumer language to best resonate with the most profitable audience.

Traditional brand positioning evolved to specifically mirror a defined target's emotional needs. Brands were given personalities that consumers would be drawn to. Brand leaders got in the business of manufacturing hearts and souls to bring their brands to life. The brands were created to be consumer avatars, designed to have the target see him or herself in the brand and fall in love.

This was the birth of inauthenticity. These are the Posers.

As social media exploded into the marketing arena, many Posers began finding themselves reluctantly pushed onto a stage to connect with consumers on a different level – one in which the brand cannot successfully engage by robotically repeating tested, consumer-approved language. Consumers now want to relate to brands on a more personal, spontaneous, and intimate level; they want to see behind the curtain.

But the Tin Man has no heart.

As if matters weren't bad enough, now these brands are being forced to show more skin than they're comfortable with as they increasingly become questioned about their motives, sources, policies, and ethics.

Feeling uncomfortably exposed, many brands have grabbed a fig

FREE RANGE
BRANDS

leaf, aligning themselves with a noble cause to borrow a sense of "purpose." But consumers can tell the difference between a superficial tactic and a core truth, so these programs tend to have little if no impact other than temporary content filler.

Today, consumers can sniff out the Posers with an intrinsic human sense that cannot be mechanically averted.

Microsoft, a brand with undeniably strong product offerings, has never been able to connect with consumers intimately like its Mac counterpart has.

After years of being portrayed as the fat, white, corporate guy, Microsoft hastily jumped into the Apple parody game mocking its competitor's culture. But the ad's lack of point or purpose, combined with its defensive voice, turned what they expected to be clever and fun into an embarrassment. With egg on its face, Microsoft quickly pulled the ad.

When a brand really doesn't know who it is, it doesn't have a compass for consumer interaction. Looking to get noticed, Hyundai tried to inject humor into its innovative message of "100% water emissions." The brand team developed what they thought would be a clever spoof of a man trying to commit suicide by sitting in a running car in his closed garage. But because Hyundai's 100% water emissions are non-toxic, the suicide attempt was unsuccessful. Get it? Sadly, Hyundai didn't. After community outrage, Hyundai pulled the ad and apologized.

Posing can often be observed in our political arena. Voter-resonating campaigns often become the Achilles Heel for the everyday politician. Campaign strategies are led by unearthing insights through focus groups, testing winning positions with the target audience, and then crafting promises or solutions that the desired audience would like to hear. But as the winds change or the message tires, politicians chase the new winning position, leaving voters with an ugly feeling of having supported a shell versus substance. The flip flopper. The chameleon; disingenuous. The candidate is left with the stench of inauthenticity that's hard to wash off.

The problem is that the campaign message is often bound and defined by solving for what is wrong versus inspiring what could be; what is missing versus what is possible. It's static, unchanging, and hooked on a problem/solution at its core. By design, it mirrors voters' tested emotions, which has great immediate appeal, but is hard to refresh in an authentic way as feelings evolve.

When you design your brand to be a mirror of your target, it's hard to have a voice of your own. Reinventing the traditional "posturing" model will sever the root that feeds brand inauthenticity.

# 3. Be a Platform

Today, a brand has to be authentic *and* relevant. Timeless *and* current. Centered *and* dynamic.

A brand has the power and opportunity to be something bigger than its functional offering or a manufactured, consumer-reflected personality. In some cases, brands are more powerful than world leaders or governments. Recognizing its responsibility, a brand must go beyond a borrowed purpose. The brands that are aware that they have this power (and responsibility) are playing on an entirely different level than the brands that are still tied to the traditional positioning and posing models. They are tapping into the new consumer energy that consumers are hungry for. Millennials want to "Feel the Bern."

Building a brand platform, rather than pushing a position, invites a community to build the momentum, rather than solving for an unmet target need. The target is invited and inspired to help manifest that vision because they subscribe to the dream, not the solution. The possibility, not the product. The obsession, not the position.

Free Range Platforming is based on conviction. What does the team behind the brand believe in? What unites the brand's community of users? Not "what does the product do?"

Rather than sharing a common product-related need and offering, Free Range Brands share a personal obsession with their consumers. This obsession can be arrived at through a variety of entry points and can transcend demographics. The brand is the obsession

NOT

the position

FREE RANGE
BRANDS

no longer the product line, it is the leader of a community. The brand defines the platform; the community creates multiple positionings that interpret the platform.

The unmet need is naturally solved by the product offerings that the brand delivers as part and parcel of driving towards a shared obsession. And as the journey unfolds, more unmet needs present themselves, which the brand can offer to the community in the form of products or services. In this way, the brand and the products, the innovation and the message, authenticity and relevancy become one. The brand evolves and innovates in a way that is authentically connected to the original product, but not necessarily functionally related.

Today's consumers must know what to expect from you. They align with ideas, movements and brands that have a powerful core; a steadfast conviction. This pervasive need is what has spawned the relatively new requirement for "Brand Purpose." But "purpose" can often be misinterpreted to mean a requirement to achieve a noble deed.

This interpretation is too narrow and strict. Brands can just as easily have a hedonistic conviction as long as it is steadfast and true to who they are and what they do. It is not a brand requirement to fix the world—the requirement is consistency, conviction, and ethics.

Urban Outfitters is consistently shocking and provocative. The requirement is not that a brand have a noble purpose; it is that it possess a distinct, unwavering, authentic truth and an adherence to a higher-order code of ethics in how it manifests that truth.

Positioning is static and unchanging. Posing is inauthentic. Platforming is progressive, renewable, and refreshing.

Will you be the Product, the Poser, or the Platform?

## UNTIL FURTHER NOTICE: BRANDING 101 CLASSES ARE CANCELLED

## ENJOY THE OUTDOORS

# II

# THE WINDS OF CHANGE

"Only a crisis, actual or perceived, produces real change ..."

"When that crisis occurs, the actions that are taken depend on the ideas that are lying around."

-Milton Friedman

# THE WINDS OF CHANGE

Technology changed everything.

Did it?

The Millennials have taken over.

Have they?

The changes we are experiencing today are fueled by far more than just new technology and young minds. What we're seeing today is a coming of age of ideas and conversations that have been happening around dinner tables for generations.

Technology didn't change us—it enabled us. We've reached a cultural tipping point. Social media has done nothing more than enabled a long-awaited power shift. It has taken the keys from the kingdom and handed it over to the consumers.

The landscape feels chaotic; one in which random acts of creative brilliance steal the show. But is that it? Luck? Timing? Creativity? Or is there a method to the madness? The answer lies in unlocking the mind behind the machine.

* * *

For the last 50 years, marketers dished it out. Consumer watchdog groups such as the Ralph Naders of the world tended to be sideline fanatics who often appealed to the fringe: the conspiracy theorists. Big companies wouldn't lie; why would they? They were the experts, the authority. Consumers didn't have the data or the facts. Trust was the alchemy that held the whole system together.

The seeds of mistrust started to sprout with the Boomers, who broke from their parents' generation, The Silent Generation. Conversations around kitchen tables led to curiosity, questions. Questions found their way to the customer call center, buried, ignored, or responded to with a form letter. But these worms of curiosity didn't die. They grew.

Boomers used their megaphones, marches, and posters to demand answers and changes on big issues that made the news and got attention. They were the first generation to speak out against institutions and governments, seeking the truth and driving for change. Vietnam, Ohio State, Apartheid, Watergate. Younger Boomers grew up to pass their values of being change agents and influencers on to their kids: the Millennials.

Besides being the digital natives, Millennials have a unique, holistic distinction from any generation that precedes them: they really like their Boomer parents. Consider these facts:

- 33% of Millennials are currently living at home;[†]
- 45% of Millennials talk with their parents on the phone daily;[†]
- Millennials enjoy closer, more friendly relationships with their parents than previous generations.[‡]

This is a radical departure from any parent-child generational relationship in history, in which kids tend to reject, rebel, or at the very least, seek to outdo or rethink how they were brought up.

Raised surrounded with endless media, Millennials had a 24/7, front-row booster seat to the world stage of unprecedented tragedy, disaster and scares. But despite it all, these kids grew up with a

† 2015 Pew Research Center
‡ Morley Winograd and Michael D. Hais, *Millennial Makeover*

Boomer-infused conviction that they had the power to be seen and heard, and the responsibility to invoke real change.

As they came of age, Web 1.0 turned into Web 2.0: User Generated Content.

Kitchen tables turned into global pulpits and a whole new mode of consumer communication hatched. The ugly wizards behind the Big Brand curtains were forced to face their consumers on a very public stage. And Mutiny by Transparency began.

It may seem like technology and social media have spurned an overnight upheaval of the world we live in. But what we're seeing is five decades of generational momentum hitting the fan. It is nothing more than kitchen table conversations finding their voice and power through a better megaphone.

What this means is Millennials aren't singlehandedly rethinking the world. They are the executors of the ideas that their parents never saw across the finish line. The baton has been passed and they are using their digital prowess to finish what their parents started.

And, in turn, we unearth a clearer picture of not just 80 million Millennials, but of 160 million people who are at the core of changing everything: the two largest generations in history working together, often still living together, and fueling and supporting each other: Boomers and Millennials.

# MUTINY by TRANSPARENCY

FREE RANGE BRANDS

## THE MODERN MINDSET

Free Range Brands are successful because they understand the modern mindset. They understand that all the new media channels are nothing more than the new kitchen table. The brand leaders who are chasing the channels just to be "on Facebook" or "on Instagram" are missing the point. It's not the "table" that matters—it's the conversation.

There are four deep-seated, cultural needs that are now emerging and fueling nearly all social engagements.

The Need for Self Expression
The Need to Influence
The Need for Relevancy
The Need for Truth

Each of these four needs impacts how consumers expect to interact with their brands. Free Range Brands understand them and consistently activate against them.

Let's explore each of the four consumer needs that have changed our marketing landscape.

# 1. THE NEED FOR SELF-EXPRESSION

Two generations ago, Boomers ignited the counter-culture movement. Self-expression defined their generation as they broke from the "Silent Generation" with experimentation, exploration, and a bold new voice. They were the force behind the upheaval of music, festivals, fashion, sex, and feminism.

Boomers infused these values in their Millennial children, encouraging them to express themselves in ways that no generation before them was enabled. Millennials are the most diverse generation yet, with approximately 43 percent being non-white.[†] Millennials don't see one way to experience the world. Fusion, mash-up, and experimentation combined with a strong desire for self expression makes standing out and being noticed more desirable than blending in.

They are the American Idol generation, energized by the spotlight, beginning at a very young age. The Result: Follow Me, Broadcast Yourself, Subscribe to my Blog, and Selfies.

The need for self-expression presents an opportunity for brands to give consumers a way to showcase their individuality through the brand.

† 2015 Pew Research Center

## 2. THE NEED TO INFLUENCE

Millennials were raised by a generation most known for its activism, fueled by a distaste for war, dirty politics, inequality, and injustice. Their parents challenged the establishment, existing laws, and leaders. They were the first generation to speak out against institutions and drive for change. Their idealism and voice helped topple governments and end wars.

Then, it was Watergate, women's liberation, and civil rights. Today, it centers on the environment, corporate responsibility, sourcing, and sustainability. Aside from their penchant for self-expression, activism is a core foundation of the "counter culture" that defined the Boomers.

It's no surprise, then, that their children have carried this value forward with a vengeance. As change-makers in the digital age, Millennials are known as the Alpha Influencers.

Their protests take a different form than the protests of the past. They are savvy at building communities to generate momentum. They are the Wiki generation.

Working parent Boomers raised their Millennial children in team environments from a very early age. Millennials have been in constant contact with others their whole lives. Even the explosive gaming cohort is often geared toward the team mentality versus the individual. This generation has an enormous capacity to work together across digital channels to mobilize and influence change.

They use their voice and dollars to be heard. Millennials see their dollars as far more than currency; they see their spending choices as a way to influence change. They know their options are wide open for finding products they need and like, and tend to utilize their funds to support or derail brands. They are more influential than any generation before them and will use social media to reshape how the world should work according to their values.

An opportunity for brands is to be more than a product or service offering, but also to be a means for a consumer to be seen and heard.

# 3. THE NEED TO BE RELEVANT

Millennials' expectation of rapid change seems to have affected their expectations for creativity and innovation in their own work lives.‡

This generation connects with brands in motion. Status quo is no longer a safe place. Everything is under review.

Emboldened by their parents, Millennials are increasingly reinventing everything from workplace culture to parenting. No longer defined by demographics, cultural norms, ethnicity, or physical proximity, Millennials relate by ideals and inspiration. They are migrating to urban life faster than any generation preceding them. They fully expect to rewrite rules, redefine standards, and drive trends.

So, being "relevant" is bigger than well-placed and well-timed marketing communications. It's more than just timely output. It is beyond new product or feature offerings, upgrades, or changes. It's simply not a one-way output. It requires integration, reexamination, or, at the very least, objective observation.

Progressive action is a Millennial's status quo. Millennials simply can't connect with brands that aren't in a constant state of motion, evaluation, and evolution.

The challenge this places on brands is how to integrate constant reinvention with a committed, steadfast purpose. This is the tightrope that today's brands must not only walk, but stretch on both extremes.

‡ US Council of Economic Advisers, Oct 2014

# 4. THE NEED FOR TRUTH

Millennials' parents were the original Truth Seekers. They still maintain a general distrust of authority and tend to educate themselves to be fully knowledgeable on issues that affect them. They pride themselves on exposing raw truths versus accommodating pretense and conventional wisdom.

Millennials too are naturally skeptical. Despite Millennial coddling inside the home, they never knew life without war, greed, or destruction. As they came of age, banks were embroiled in scandal, social security headed towards bankruptcy, and the American dream of home ownership began to fade. They are not inclined to trust any large institution, such as the Church or their bank. Growing up, they bridged two centuries, imploding economies, and ongoing wars. Buildings were bombed, terrorism flourished, and security lines and cameras became a fact of life.

Twenty-somethings have been hard hit by these economic times. They are the first generation to inherit an economy in decline. More heavily debt ridden than any previous generation, today's average college graduate is emerging with approximately $24,000 in educational and other loans. Only 54 percent of adults between 18 and 24 are currently employed, according to a recent study by the Pew Research Center, the lowest since the government started collecting the data in 1948 and the highest unemployment rate of all age groups. Combined with heavy debt burdens, many 20-somethings have moved back home with their Boomer parents.

As a result, Millennials' trust issues reign supreme. This generation doesn't want to relinquish financial control to any large institution or government and wants to depend on themselves. Sixty-six percent of Millennials want to start their own business.[‡]

What does it mean for brands? Both generations share a penchant for truth and transparency. Brands must work very hard to connect with them in authentic and genuine ways.

† Millennials at Work, Bentley University, November 2014

# III

# MEET THE NEW CONSUMER

# THE FREE RANGE ARENA

Primary consumer needs range from ***Expressing Oneself*** to ***Influencing Others.***

At the same time, consumers expect Brands to balance an unwavering ***Authenticity*** while being ***Hyper-Relevant*** in a fast-changing environment.

When Consumer Needs (Express Self and Influence Others) intersect with Brand Requirements (Authenticity and Hyper-Relevancy) a framework for consumer / brand relationships emerges.

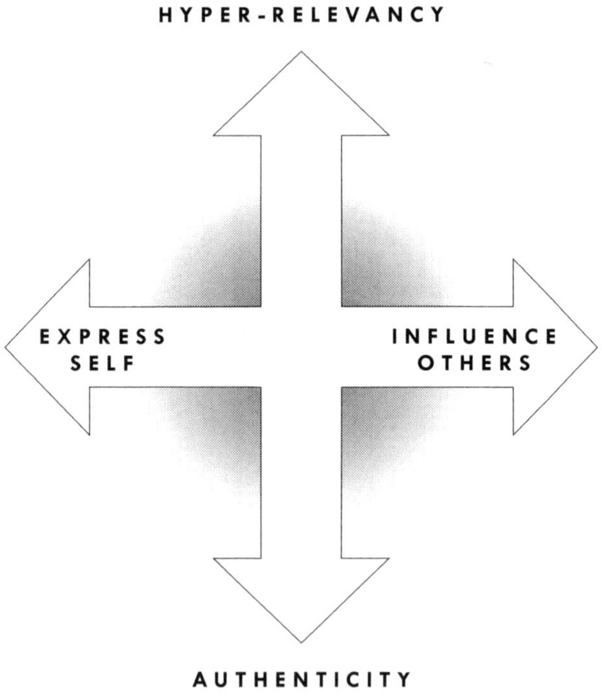


FREE RANGE BRANDS

# THE NEW CONSUMERS

This framework reveals four ways consumers interact with brands. These interactions can be personified by consumer archetypes: Lords, Lovers, Hackers, and Hawks.

These are the four new personas that brands must appeal to in all marketing activities. Understanding their needs and how to market to them is the foundation of Free Range Branding.

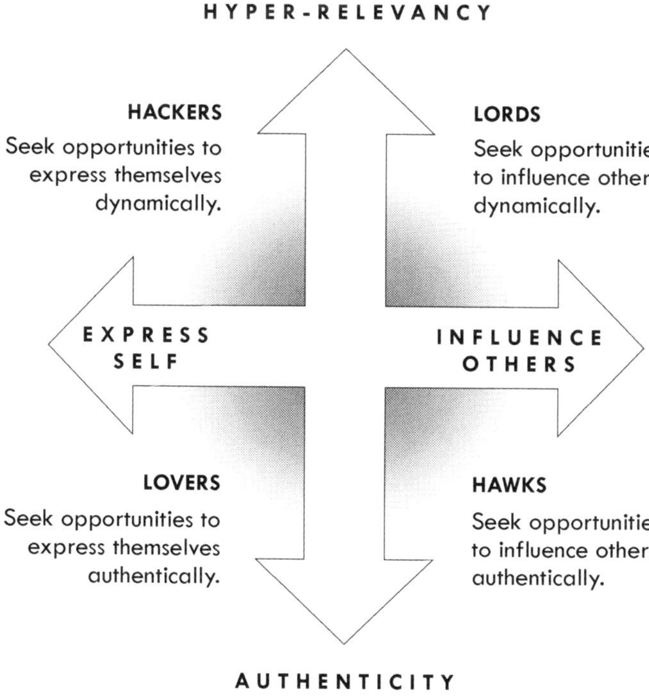

# LORDS

## DYNAMIC INFLUENCERS

FREE RANGE
BRANDS

# LORDS

When a generation of alpha-influencers mixes with full-on, instant access to information, the unknown, the unseen, or something irretrievably "missed" has incredible value. Sports. Live debates. Spoilers. First to find.

Enter the Lords.

Lords are an evolution of the coveted big-name "influencer." Lords are found in micro-communities, curating smaller, yet deeper territories of influence with highly expectant followers. Lords can be provocative kids with smartphones, dog lovers with GoPros, moms with Facebook pages, and food lovers with kitchen webcams.

Unlike the pre-age influencer, Lords cannot be targeted with overt brand messages.

Discovery is their currency and Lords are on the hunt for this currency to retain their ruling over their self-defined sphere of influence with their goal of expanding their followers. Constant reinvention and re-imagining therefore becomes critical.

A Lord's status is powered by what he or she finds. Lords trade on a black market of information not readily accessible to the masses. They seek hyper-relevant, yet-to-be-shared information to bring to their followers.

Brands can ride these social under-currents by making content more interesting and inaccessible to the masses, yet discoverable by the right Lords. Information must be harder to find, bite-sized, and easy to serve out when the Lord deems it worthy.

Brands can attract and court their Lords with the currency of Discovery.

# LOVERS

## AUTHENTIC SELF-EXPRESSION

FREE RANGE BRANDS

# LOVERS

Channel and functional ubiquity has led to product commoditization, creating a powerful opportunity for brands to connect on an entirely different level.

Consumers want to have a profound love affair with your brand. Anything short of that is a commodity. If they can't absolutely love you, they'll leave you as soon as something better or cheaper comes along. And it will. It doesn't get any simpler than that.

Lovers seek to align their identities with brands that resonate more powerfully than solving for an unmet functional need. They seek brands that reflect their souls. When a brand's authenticity syncs with a consumer's self identity, a Lover is born.

Lovers' currency is Chemistry.

Building Chemistry with Lovers will create powerful bonds for brands.

# HACKERS

## DYNAMIC SELF-EXPRESSION

FREE RANGE BRANDS

# HACKERS

Combining a keen sense of being noticed, a vengeance for assertion, and an unprecedented level of technological proficiency has uncorked a generation of brand-jackers who can't be put back in the bottle. They are fueled by self-expression of individuality, a desire to experiment, an expectation of two-way dialogue, and a world view of diversity, stimulating unconventional mash-up & fusion.

Meet the Hackers. They expect to cross boundaries that you perhaps once thought were sacred. They feel an inherent right to manhandle your brand. They feel it is for them, and that they have every right to be able to play with it. They want to invent their own solutions and assert their voice in the marketplace. They simply expect to create their own version of a brand that works uniquely for them.

For brand leaders who are hardwired for ultimate brand control, the Hackers are a force to be reckoned with. Co-creation, crowd-creation, personalization, and customization ... they're more gropey than what we're used to. You want your brand to live in this world? Stop controlling. Let go. Give the Hackers access.

Hackers' currency is Interactivity.

# HAWKS

## AUTHENTIC INFLUENCERS

FREE RANGE
BRANDS

# HAWKS

Hawks have a pent-up need for Justice. Transparency has unleashed a long-standing, collective score to settle among generations threading all the way up through Boomers. Fueled by years of growing organizational mistrust and victimization (financial, government, pharma, FDA, Catholic Church, Wall Street, and the list goes on), transparency has not only opened the floodgates of Hawks' thirst for knowledge, it's unleashed a force that can't be stopped. Hawks finally know they are in control, and they have the digital pulpit to voice it.

As empowered influencers, Hawks expect everyone, especially large corporations, to have some level of responsibility to the greater good. A token good deed promotion only insults the watchful Hawks. A higher-order brand dimension of philosophical alignment is a mandate beyond a marketing program. Consumers now know their options are wide open for finding products they need—they will vote with their dollars to have a greater effect than just buying a functional solution.

With their dollars, Consumers are funding the future choices your brand makes. They're supporting you and fueling you. They're investors in your vision. They take this very personally. They must be able to trust, inside and out, that you are what you say you are and you will use the profits wisely. Any sniff of suspicion and you're going to be put on a very public stage for questioning.

The Hawks are a rabid force and can unleash quickly without warning.

The Currency of the Hawks is Validity.

# These Consumers activate the brand narrative ...

Lords SHARE the story;

Hackers ILLUSTRATE the story;

Hawks VALIDATE the story;

Lovers SEE THEMSELVES in the story.

# IV

# BUILDING BRAND CURRENCY

# BUILDING BRAND CURRENCY

Today's brand-building game is played in an entirely new arena and demands a new mode of brand engagement.

Free Range Brands embrace our new reality by fixing their sights on goals that are beyond product-centric or need-based—ideals that communities can participate in, perhaps even lead. Elevating to a higher plane to avoid the turbulence or headwinds. It takes courage, commitment, and practice. Free Range Brands can travel and explore without losing their way; they don't get lost redefining themselves as the market changes to keep up with social or content marketing efforts.

The brands that are thriving in this new world have made the shift from the old-world model of planning for control to the new-world model of planning for unpredictability. The shift is strategically profound. It is one from building Brand Equity to one of building Brand Currency.

To build a Free Range Brand requires Currency. Brand Currency buys agility and relevant reinvention. This is a sharp distinction from traditional brands that are still focused on building brand Equity, often through repetitive messaging. Equity is static; Currency is dynamic. Currency buys fluidity in unpredictable environments. Currency allows for agility and responsiveness.

Brands that aren't trading in brand currency are continuing the old models of pre-programming for a pre-determined destination. Sometimes it works. But more often, the brand leaders are finding themselves constantly reprogramming and eroding brand equity.

Free Range Brands operate in a more fluid, agile method. They prepare by building currency.

Each consumer Archetype values a distinct Currency:

Lords value Discovery.
Lovers value Chemistry.
Hackers value Interactivity.
Hawks value Validity.

Evaluating and selecting which marketing programs to build into a plan can be simplified by focusing on tactics that build currency.

Only four major currencies exist. Are any of your programs building currency? Are your programs working cohesively to holistically build all four? Or are they too heavy in one?

Let's explore what successful programs look like to build each currency.

# DISCOVERY

## *CURRENCY OF THE LORDS*

Go Micro

Roam

Elude

Delight

Inspire

FREE RANGE BRANDS

## CURRENCY OF THE LORDS

# DISCOVERY

With so much information, Lords are curating smaller, yet deeper territories of influence. Discovery is the modern form of competition or one-upmanship and has great value to today's influential Lords. When brand messages are overt and ubiquitous, it robs the Lords of the opportunity to be the "bringers" of news.

In the Broadcast era, a stand-alone campaign could run for years. But today, brand communication is better served up in smaller, more frequent and current, devourable bites to allow for repurposing by the Lords. Creating this currency for the Lords means deconstructing overt messages into covert shareables.

There are endless ways to build the currency of Discovery to ignite your Lords.

Let's take a look at some different ways to think about Discovery.

renew
refresh
reinvent

## DISCOVERY: CURRENCY OF THE LORDS

### GO MICRO

In today's economy, one big event doesn't have the inertia it once had. Hello, Goodbye, Pokemon Go. Size just doesn't matter anymore as even the biggest hit is quickly forgotten and replaced by the next, which, by the way, could equally be a tiny event.

Micro-interactions are tiny opportunities of engagement that brands can tap into or create to delight the Lords.

One of Trader Joe's most valuable assets is its high currency of micro-innovation, ongoing roll-outs of new fusions, flavors and creations, sampled daily, in-store. Shoppers who frequent the store know there will always be something new and interesting at Trader Joe's. These little Easter eggs of innovation are never obvious, but rather nestled throughout the store for shoppers to discover on their everyday shopping journeys. Seasonal or trendy, Trader Joe's finds ways to make the everyday shopping experience special, talk-worthy, and share-worthy among Foodie Lords.

Oreo celebrated its 100th birthday with a "Daily Twist," posting 100 days of artwork made from the iconic cookie, commemorating a relevant topic of the day, a pop culture fact, a world event, or a holiday. It effectively unbundled a big creative idea into small, ongoing shareables, engaging Lords to pick up and share the artistic icons that speak to them uniquely.

In late 2016, NBC Universal signed a deal to create exclusive, original content for Snapchat in the form of mini TV shows. Not repurposed versions of existing shows, but mini-shows made to be mini. In the old world, bigger was better. Today, micro-niche is where it's at.

ROAM
Don't Root
FREE RANGE

## DISCOVERY: CURRENCY OF THE LORDS

### ROAM, DON'T ROOT.

Back in the day, partnering with another brand was a long-term engagement that required a heavy amount of up-front consideration. Not anymore.

In a surprise move, Kit Kat jumped into bed with Android. On the surface, Kit Kat and Android would seemingly have no reason to play together. But the move reinforced a natural chemistry that fit Kit Kat's authenticity: its unique form.

Kit Kat 4.4 is highlighted as "Beautifully crafted for a multi-sensory experience ... with adjustable orientation (portrait or landscape) ... global coverage ... only 10 millimeters thick ... and available in 2MegaBite, 4MegaBite or ChunkyBite."

A1 went through its divorce with Steak, deciding it really preferred a more open relationship with food. Dropping "Steak" from its "A1 Steak Sauce" name, it's now jumping into bed with pork, tofu, fish, and green beans, creating new uses and ideas for A1 Lovers.

Unlike the pre-digital era of long-term partnerships, today's partnerships are more like flings. H&M and Jimmy Choo, Patagonia & beer, Ford & Cuervo, and the Heineken 100. Some are great; some are just a flash in the pan. But sitting on the sidelines, wed to one partner forever is for the Tethered Brands that leave us uninspired.

So go ahead, put your peanut butter in someone else's chocolate.

be covert

FREE RANGE
BRANDS

## DISCOVERY: CURRENCY OF THE LORDS

# ELUDE

What do food trucks, Snapchat, Facebook Live, and Periscope have in common? They're fleeting; ephemeral. In a world where every brand is bombarding us with their messages, being elusive has great value when discovered by the Lords.

When J. Crew decided to elevate the image of their menswear line, they took over an old New York bar with no branded signage and instead retained the old neon sign that was still hanging: "Liquor Store." Inside dressing rooms they hung curated paintings and photography, and the men's boutique was filled with a limited offering of J. Crew's premium offerings. Liquor Store remains one of J. Crew's most successful stores today. Travel and fashion Lords are sure to share this find with their confidants.

DayBreaker is an underground urban party that pops up in unsuspecting locations at a most unusual time: before work. Starting with early morning yoga and progressing into a full-blown dance party, the concept has been built entirely by appealing to the Lords via Discovery with last-minute emails revealing where and when the next pre-work pop-up party will be. The trend has spread quickly and globally, almost completely under the radar.

Pop-up stores, real-time events that can't be recorded, only experienced by those who were there. This is the stuff that has great value to the Lords.

Delete this page after reading.

## DISCOVERY: CURRENCY OF THE LORDS

### DELIGHT

Discovery isn't limited to big events or significant innovation. It can be as simple as unexpected, delightful brand experiences.

Amazing customer service has been the differentiator for more than one brand, but ceases to wear old.

Warby Parker, known for stylish, affordable eyewear served up in a smart, socially responsible package, credits its success most profoundly to the company's exceptional customer service. They believe their early success was heavily attributed to replying personally to every customer via email to create a customer service experience worth talking about by the style Lords. And today, the founders still believe that creating exceptional customer experiences is the simple secret to their success.

One of the most talked-about brands that has scored big with traveling Lords is Delta. By tweeting your traveling troubles to @DeltaAssist, you'll get quick, friendly help via Twitter—even to your most challenging travel woes, a nice discovery for these Lords to share with other travelers.

Chobani's explosive growth is also highly back-end driven. The brand has a customer loyalty team that answers more than 9,000 emails and calls a month, often responding with handwritten notes. "We want each individual to feel like a personal connection to our brand," says Hamdi Ulukaya, fouder and CEO of Chobani. And the protein-hungry Lords eat it up.

Free Range Brands know every opportunity to delight a customer creates far-reaching momentum beyond that experience, often spread by the Lords who love to share unexpected experiences.

## DISCOVERY: CURRENCY OF THE LORDS

# INSPIRE

Rather than relying on traditional campaign-driven broadcasts, the Obama brand was largely built by inspiring the Lords to influence a target.

Obama was facing poor "brand" perceptions among elderly Jewish voters in Florida, a key swing state. The team identified their Lords, the micro-community of influencers who could be inspired to take on the task of changing the views of Florida's elderly Jewish voters. In this case, the Lords were Jewish grandchildren living around the county who were Obama fans.

Droga5 and the Jewish Council for Education and Research teased out a YouTube ad featuring Sarah Silverman, called "The Great Schlep." When discovered by the young, Obama-supporting Lords, they were presented with a clear charge and helpful talking points. The grandchildren were also given specific suggestions on how to approach and navigate the conversations with their grandparents.

The talking points were downloaded over 200,000 times and The Great Schlep received over 350 million media impressions, tipping the vote in favor of Obama in Florida: 51 to 49 percent. By inspiring the Lords, Obama received the highest elderly Jewish vote in 30 years.

Identifying, inspiring, and facilitating action for the Lords is a big reason Obama was named "Marketer of the Year" by AdAge and "Brand Obama" by Fast Company.

Who are your Lords? What do they need to help you change beliefs and behaviors for your target audience?

## IGNITING DISCOVERY

# COURT YOUR LORDS

Your Lords are influencers to your target. Sometimes they are your target; sometimes they are not. But they always influence your target.

1. Identify your Lords. Think about your target consumer and go further … who and where is your target getting their information, inspiration, and influence? What are they reading, doing, who are they following? Where do they go? Where are they when they are not thinking about you?

2. You've defined your Lords. What can you bring to these people to make them more valuable to their audience that they can't otherwise access? How can you help them build their brand, business, or following? What information, ideas, or insights can you provide them?

3. Now, let's identify Lords that are outside your category. What other brands, outside your industry, share your values? Think beyond the obvious. Pick five businesses outside your category and ask yourself: if brands were people, which brand would your brand be friends with? Why? What values/interests do they share?

4. Now engage those Lords. What would those brands have in common to talk about? Don't think about product relationship, but think in terms of a cocktail conversation if both

brands were human. How can you engage in their forums and have a voice, for no reason other than to inspire, delight, or surprise? How can you show up in an unintrusive way, requiring nothing in exchange?

5. Every interaction is an opportunity for an unexpected Discovery waiting to be shared. When your customers need you, are you consistently there for them, making your interaction exceptional and talk-worthy? How are you going above and beyond what they would expect?

# CHEMISTRY

## CURRENCY OF THE LOVERS

Just Be It

Seduce

Humanize

Channel it

FREE RANGE BRANDS

## CURRENCY OF THE LOVERS

# CHEMISTRY

Consumers have a profound need for authentic self-expression. Forging Chemistry requires a brand to establish a platform that allows for a consumer's authentic self to be expressed through the brand.

Now, more than ever, consumers look to their brands to say something distinct about themselves and who they are, express what is important to them and, in some cases, even stimulate conversation. It's less about blending in and belonging, and more about standing true and being acknowledged.

Chemistry can be built by laddering up brand positioning to be more transcendent, preparing a brand to be a force of authentic expression for the Lovers.

A brand that can build Chemistry is one that does not let itself be defined by what it does, but by its obsession. It looks forward, not backwards.

A Lover is drawn into the story not as a target demographic, but as one who shares the dream, vision, interest, or curiosity. The obsession becomes inspiring to the Lovers and Chemistry is sparked. This is the basis of a higher connection.

## CHEMISTRY: CURRENCY OF THE LOVERS

# JUST BE IT

So, how does a brand that is void of backstory, purpose, or dimension create a platform that rivals the brands that are dripping with that oh-so-desirable sauce of authenticity, conviction, passion, and relevancy? Let's face it—most brands were either born in the problem/solution era of brand development or simply evolved that way.

As desirable and necessary as it is, an obsession beyond a functional offering is very often elusive. Building Chemistry is all about embracing a core essence that can be expressed in a true, authentic sense, inspiring identification with the Lovers.

Some small brands start with an obsession, overflowing with an authentic brand narrative and passionate backstory. Most large brands were never built or established to have much beyond a corporate, functional proposition. Some very old brands, feeling tethered to their past or handcuffed to a sizeable existing market, feel constrained to even consider creating a more profound platform because it requires reinvention and are afraid of alienating some of their existing consumers. Perhaps they feel there is little to work with; or, often, they believe they are far more interesting to their consumers than they realize.

Let's start by not getting too hung up on what our brands really are or aren't.

We tend to trap ourselves within the confines of whatever established equities we can excavate to reverse-engineer a contrived "purpose." The result often comes off like a bad comb-over.

The reality is that it simply doesn't matter what our brands presently stand for, if anything. Nor does it matter if we have baggage, despite our fears. We have more options to build a compelling narrative than we think we do.

The Adidas brand was looking like a forgotten brand by 2014, having been outclassed by both Nike and Under Armour, especially in the North American market. But by 2016, Adidas fueled an unexpected, come-from-behind rush, outpacing the growth of both brands. Adidas tapped into the cultural zeitgeist with its "Never Follow" campaign and boldly laid claim to a belief system rooted in independence and non-conformity.

"The other brands are very traditional in how they tell their story," said North America President Mark King. "We are deeply engaged in society and culture and bring that together in performance and style. That's why this brand has become cool almost overnight."

Adidas didn't stop there. Lords are trading on the currency of non-stop Adidas activity while Hackers can get their creativity on and make their own version of the brand, both engaging along shared values of independent style and self expression.

Free Range Brands, like Adidas, know that creating Lovers is not about hawking product, but linking product values to audience values. All you have to do is stake it and claim it, and it's yours for the taking.

What are you waiting for? It's a choice. Just be it.

SEDUCE
don't solve
FREE RANGE
BRANDS

## CHEMISTRY: CURRENCY OF THE LOVERS

## SEDUCE

Most brands simply can't stop talking about themselves. What they do. Why you should consider them. Why they are better or different. How they'll solve your problems. Or, worse, they do nothing but plaster billboards all over town, arrogantly screaming their brand name. (Lookin' at you, Yahoo!)

The brands that strike the real chords share a common trait: they don't talk about themselves. They don't tell the "brand narrative" but, rather, they reflect the audience's story. This creates huge currency with the Lovers.

A Free Range Brand leads with seduction. It connects with its target by its behaviors, not its chatter. It reflects a quality, value, or obsession that consumers share, and then gives them access to that through the brand's actions, interactions, values, and engagement.

In 2016, Heineken stunned the marketing world by elevating its long-running ***Open your World*** platform all the way up to embrace the heart of the global organization.

Heineken's marketing has been on a long run of slaying hearts worldwide. But the team didn't rest on its laurels. In 2016, they took it to a level few organizations have yet to go (yet all must): to the world of unsuspecting future employees who might be dreaming of a better life.

While all other organizations walk like sheep through the traditional rigors of recruiting, Heineken turned the tables and put the heart of the company – the people, the culture, and the mindset – on the table and

"Seducers are never self absorbed. Their gaze is directed outward, not inward. Self absorption is anti-seductive; it is a sign of insecurity."

*-The Art of Seduction, by Robert Greene*

let the world take it in. No pushing stale, empty messages of career progression, job descriptions, work/life balance, and mission statements. Heineken's recruiting campaign entices Lovers to "follow their heart," to a culture (not a company) that will allow them to "Go Places," wherever that may be. It's not a predefined destination. Seduction doesn't solve problems with finite solutions, but lets the audience imagine a world with themselves in it.

Employers can learn from consumer marketers on building brands to make the leap from being an employer, to being a Free Range employer brand. This requires a re-imagination of communications from functional benefits such as job descriptions, career paths, and pay grades, to experiential platforms that engage emotionally.

Heineken has set the bar for all Free Range Brands, bringing the brand's heart so far forward, it literally set a company of more than 250 brands afloat into dreamland.

Now, that's seduction.

## CHEMISTRY: CURRENCY OF THE LOVERS

# HUMANIZE

Chemistry is all about capturing the hearts, not the minds. About turning products into friends, humanizing them to become a force of connection.

GE humanized what otherwise would be a complex brand that produces products ranging from aviation to consumer appliances, healthcare, and power. GE brilliantly connected all its divisions through the platform of "Imagination at Work," humanizing the brand and capturing the hearts and minds of an audience that ranges from the most technical to the most general. GE uses humor, personal connection and inspiration throughout a range of platforms including YouTube, Facebook, Instagram, Tumblr, Vine & Snapchat, showcasing the mind-blowing aspects of their brand without delving too deeply into the technical aspects.

"We have more than a million followers on Facebook, and they love to hear about innovation," says a GE Marketing Director. "We don't talk about how we built a great gas turbine that delivers return on investment. That isn't going to engage people on that platform. But we might discuss a new type of material we're thinking about or crowd-source ideas which do keep people engaged."

GE's Facebook posts revolve around fun, engaging questions, eye-catching images, and fascinating facts about the brand that are share-worthy for the general consumer or enthusiast. Yet it still connects with the most technical audiences in very targeted ways.

## CHEMISTRY: CURRENCY OF THE LOVERS

# CHANNEL IT

Sometimes, a common enemy can spark Chemistry. Powerful affairs can swirl in the riptides, waiting for a leader to unleash them. Igniting these connections doesn't often center on the values or needs you and your audience share, but rather, on what you both potentially reject.

Southern Comfort broke molds when the "Whatever's Comfortable" campaign reignited the stagnant brand by tapping into the counter-culture of the dominant trends of martini cocktail couture and single-malt stuffiness.

As the big shave brands cat scratched each other with never-ending razor innovation, Dollar Shave Club disrupted the category by asking: "Do you think your razor needs a vibrating handle, a flashlight, a backscratcher and 10 blades?"

Vice built a $4 billion media empire by standing for just about everything traditional news media didn't: Gonzo-style reporting by young, passionate, tattooed Millennials who were striving to engage an audience with impactful storytelling. The brand was marginalized by traditional news media because of its offbeat approach and casual dress style that didn't fit with "respectable" journalism.

Vice Founder Shane Smith built the news empire by staying true to an unconventional approach that scored big with Millennials. "The BBC isn't going to give a 23-year-old kid straight out of college $10 million to make a TV show–but we are. It's about taking risks."

Now, as traditional media is struggling to hang on to an audience, Vice is the fastest growing news channel among Millennials because it speaks to them directly and authentically.

When Millennials entered parenthood, helicopter parenting trends were in full throttle. But a small site called Babble tapped into a nascent undercurrent:

"We can't find a magazine or community that speaks to us as new parents. Every publication we encounter presents procreation as a cute and cuddly experience, all pink and powder blue, at best an interior decorating opportunity, at worst a housekeeping challenge. None of it is true to the experience we are having."

Babble grew to win major awards as a top website, and was since acquired by Disney. The site exposed the raw honesty of parenting, giving other brands permission to expose old clichés and question long-held standards and expectations. This ignited a current that other brands rode:

Tommee Tippee (maker of baby products) began telling new moms to take all that unwanted parenting advice they're getting and wipe their baby's butt with it. "Take a Deep Breath and Trust Yourself" #ParentOn.

Similac put itself in the explosive mommy crosshairs of the breastfeeding versus formula debate, beautifully anesthetizing the conflict and re-opening the door for formula acceptance, a daunting task during the climate in which it launched.

Are you just running with the trends with everyone else? Powerful forces exist that need a voice to ignite them. Can your brand channel that electricity?

## IGNITING CHEMISTRY

# LURE YOUR LOVERS

Lovers connect with brands that allow their authentic selves to be seen through the brand. How does your brand attract Lovers?

1. What is your obsession? This is the foundation of your platform. You aren't required to be the voice of a noble purpose. You can just as wonderfully be the voice of the antagonist or the hedonist.
2. How is your brand attracting like-minded people? How is it reflecting their values versus professing its own?
3. How is your brand modeling your platform? Not just with words, but with actions? Not just in what it does, but in what it stands for?
4. What human DNA does your brand have? If you have defined values or principles, how would they translate into a human personality? Take that personality and use it in your tone and how you engage with the world. Find like-minded personality brands and connect. Demonstrate that personality in the choices you make and the marketing activities you select.
5. How is your brand connected to others outside your target who share your values? Engaging beyond your customers along shared values is what makes the difference between a marketed brand and an authentic force.

# INTERACTIVITY

## CURRENCY OF THE HACKERS

Let Go

Converse

Reach Out

Hand Over the Keys

Invite

FREE RANGE BRANDS

## CURRENCY OF THE HACKERS

# INTERACTIVITY

Consumers today don't see one way to experience the world. Self-expression has led to co-creation, crowd-creation, brand-jacking, mash-up, and experimentation. Brands that don't "let go" and let consumers play with their brands are risking losing relevance by missing the opportunity for engagement.

Hackers thrive on dynamic self expression. A brand that can create entry points for consumer/brand interaction will be embraced by the Hackers.

Every marketer should look at every dollar spent and ask themselves the question: is there a way to involve our community in this? One-way messages have a shelf life, no matter how great they are.

## INTERACTIVITY: CURRENCY OF THE HACKERS

# LET GO

The signature move of the Hackers is to show up without an invitation. This is how most brands initially meet their Hackers. Are you prepared to engage?

In today's world, brands are challenged to interact with consumers in ways that can range anywhere from uncomfortable to illegal. Brand images get distorted, brand positionings are undermined, and brand personalities become inconsistent.

When IKEA was faced with an increasingly "intrusive" community proudly calling themselves IKEA Hackers, IKEA had a choice to make. IKEA Hackers share a passion for using the simplicity and modular nature of IKEA products to create unique, one-of-a-kind pieces of furniture. The global community congregates on ikeahackers.net to showcase and demonstrate how to recreate each unique design. In turn, more IKEA hacking businesses have emerged, (Bemz, Panyl, Superfront, and Prettypegs), selling hacking accessories to further customize and reinvent standard IKEA furniture.

IKEA's response was to issue a cease-and-desist order, demanding that the IKEA logo, the blue and yellow color scheme or anything trademarked by the company, including the ikeahackers.net domain name, be taken down.

Jules Yapp, the owner of the site said, "I felt slapped by the person I loved and thought I was doing my best for. I wish IKEA could have looked at it from my side of the fence—that the site has generated tons of publicity and goodwill for their brand, which they did not pay a cent for." In fact, "Jules" even hacked her name from the Jules Chair from IKEA. Her real name is Mei Mei.

Free Range Brands know that a Hacker's motive isn't an attack, but rather the truest expression of love and following that could possibly exist.

IKEA has since come around and is embracing its Hackers, integrating the hacking culture into its own with internal hack-a-thons and hacked furniture on display in its design center. IKEA now looks to the community to glean consumer insights and innovation ideas to improve its own offerings.

THE
BRAND-JACKERS
ARE HERE.
Wine
Wine
LET THEM IN
FREE RANGE
BRANDS

## INTERACTIVITY: CURRENCY OF THE HACKERS

### CONVERSE

Not all brands are capable of or set up for a lot of tangible interaction. But that shouldn't stop you from connecting with your Hackers. Hackers are highly conversational. Simply elevating regular, two-way communication will build great currency with the Hackers. Whether it's responding to social media posts or proactively launching programs that require communication, Hackers love to talk.

Once struggling, Taco Bell went on to achieve a feat that few fast-food chains can accomplish today: creating Millennial Lovers. Taco Bell didn't bore the Lords by talking endlessly about its tacos. It didn't enrage the Hawks by pretending to be the authentic Mexican experience.

Instead, the brand scaled this mountain by tapping into the emerging Hackers early on; Taco Bell was one of the first brands to truly build currency in Interactivity through conversation…and that meant evolving from one-way brand messaging to two-way, real-time consumer dialogue.

At a time when the chain looked to be future roadkill, Taco Bell took the fast food industry by the horns. While others were hiding from the fast food obesity Hawks, Taco Bell shifted away from those conversations and locked in on conversations that interested Millennial Hackers. The brand jumped on trends and real-time conversations with a bold voice full of personality, igniting endless Taco Bell

*tune in*

FREE RANGE
BRANDS

mini-conversations. The result was a humanized brand that spawned millions of Lovers.

Today, the brand continues to forge new ground in finding ways to monitor and scale its user-generated content across its social channels through witty replies, casual conversation, and clever whims.

And Taco Bell doesn't limit its interaction to the Hackers. Taco Bell likes to surprise its Lords, keeping the brand fresh for sharing.

Rather than simply announce its new app to all its loyal Lovers, Taco Bell effectively caught the attention of the Lords by launching a surprise social media blackout. All Taco Bell social channels were blocked and replaced with a black screen that read:

THE NEW WAY TO TACO BELL ISN'T ON
[TWITTER/INSTAGRAM/FACEBOOK/TUMBLR ...].
IT'S #ONLYINTHEAPP.

The Hackers sprung into action, diving in and downloading the new app to try it. App downloads immediately hit #1 in the food and beverage section of Apple's app store.

While online food ordering through an app wasn't revolutionary, the way the brand executed the shift was by making it elusive and then experiential, successfully activating the Lords and the Hackers.

It effectively engaged young Hackers to participate in leading the dynamic brand evolution versus being followers of a static promotion or sideline observers of a new "ordering tool."

The lesson? Don't be a tool.

# NO MASTERS

FREE RANGE BRANDS

CO
CREATE
FREE RANGE

## INTERACTIVITY: CURRENCY OF THE HACKERS

# REACH OUT

Hackers like to go beyond the package and access the brand in other ways. Brands that can find ways to reach beyond the shelf or the ad and interact with consumers more personally will do well with the Hackers.

Chobani jumped off the shelf and opened its first Chobani Bar in SOHO, creating a full-on yogurt immersion and communal space bringing the brand to life in ways it couldn't achieve on shelf. Inside the store, "yogurt masters" are there to delight customers with freshly inspired yogurt creations and exotic toppings on the base of Chobani yogurt. Toppings include gourmet dark chocolate flakes, Turkish pistachios, orange segments, mint, and clover honey. Sweet or savory, Chobani gives the Hackers a high-touch way to experience the brand. Since then, we've seen Kellogg's cereal, Moleskin notebooks, and Harley Davidson all engage their Hackers to experience their brands in their own branded cafes.

The smart retailers are transforming their spaces to cater to the Hackers. Evolving from old-school merchandising to a new model that drips of interactivity—real, old fashioned, human interactivity. Instead of competing on price and availability, the smart retailers are increasingly using the brick and mortar advantage to showcase their unique personality and philosophy to become ambassadors of lifestyle trends. The brands that can engage with their retailers to bring experiences to life will do well.

# *be the* VEHICLE

FREE RANGE
BRANDS

## INTERACTIVITY: CURRENCY OF THE HACKERS

# HAND OVER THE KEYS

This new culture of consumers is bound to tackle unprecedented change. They are in control of choosing who's on their team. They don't just want to co-create your brand. They want to co-create a new world. And you can join them if you don't serve up a canned solution.

When presidents and international leaders couldn't find peace or connection among countries at odds, Coke did. And shared it with the world. When Coke placed video vending machines in India and Pakistan, the brand turned on a global channel watched by the world.

When people of each country looked in and saw a face from the other side looking back, Coke inspired them to wave, dance, or smile. In return, the vending machine would dispense a free Coke to each side. The world watched as Coke inspired connections that bypassed governments. Coke became the platform that made the consumer and global community the heroes, enabling them to tell and view a much bigger story.

The new Free Range Brand is not the destination; it is the vehicle. Superbrands will no longer be created by a mastermind behind the curtain, seeking to control the story. They will not survive seeking to captivate a herd of brand ambassadors to manufacture awareness and mass-produce popularity. They will be motivated by a vision larger than an unmet product-related need. They will recognize their role in our rapidly evolving culture: to listen, understand, and serve.

A BRAND
FOR THE PEOPLE

FREE RANGE
BRANDS

## INTERACTIVITY: CURRENCY OF THE HACKERS

# INVITE

Every program a brand launches is an opportunity to invite the Hackers to participate. Inviting participation is a natural way to shift the center of attention from your brand to your consumer, creating a strong sense of ownership.

Brands can do this through many different entry points – from packaging, to promotions, and even to media campaigns.

For the 2016 holiday season, Godiva created a box of chocolates that kept on giving. Each box opened to two mini-boxes inside: one to enjoy and one to gift. The packaging kept going, as each box revealed two smaller sets of mini-boxes, all with the same convention. Rather than just selling a box of holiday chocolates, Godiva's packaging invited friends to participate in sharing the chocolatey joy.

Inviting participation can be activated by rethinking regular promotions. Rather than the same old, annual Back-to-School campaign, Target invited students to apply to direct, create, and perform in the nationally televised campaign.

Throwing down the gauntlet leading up to the Super Bowl, Snickers teased viewers with a small bite of creative satisfaction by holding the end of its YouTube spot hostage until viewers collectively generated 2.5 million engagements before kick-off, at which point the brand released the full spot to ravenous fans.

Inviting participation ignites your Hackers and sparks your Lovers, ramping up the sense of intense and personal brand ownership.

IGNITING INTERACTIVITY

# ENGAGE YOUR HACKERS

Calling all Hackers! Your Hackers would like to use your brand to express their individuality. Hackers' antics often get discovered by Lords.

1. Who is engaging with your brand now? How are they engaging? How can you take that engagement to another level that might help the Hackers get noticed? That's what they want.

2. How can you turn one-way messages into two-way dialogue?

3. How can your brand get people to physically interact with it experientially before purchasing it? Think beyond experiencing the actual product, but experiencing what the product stands for. Think beyond sampling and into creating experiences and communities that share an interest.

4. How can you turn your existing marketing activities into interactive activities? Can you involve your community to turn promotional marketing into communal engagement?

5. How can you invite people to help create the future of your brand?

# VALIDITY

*CURRENCY OF THE HAWKS*

Be Prepared

Know Your Truth

Practice It

Adapt

Harness

FREE RANGE BRANDS

## VALIDITY: CURRENCY OF THE HAWKS

# VALIDITY

Full access to all information has great value to today's alpha-influencers, who are naturally skeptical, distrustful, and eager to use transparency to generate momentum.

Corporate responsibility is now cost of entry. A brand's authentic connection to the cause it supports has become the new standard.

Corporate responsibility extends beyond good social citizenship and do-good tactical programs to internal and organizational belief systems and behaviors. Integrity of commitments is what matters.

Brand Authenticity will be validated or exposed by any organizational or behavioral inconsistencies to what the brand is expected to stand for.

# THE POWER OF

# ONE

FREE RANGE BRANDS

## VALIDITY: CURRENCY OF THE HAWKS

# BE PREPARED

One student. One activist. One voice.

One 23-year-old Millennial named Ed Snowden.

One post, one parody ad.

One low paycheck from McDonalds.

One YouTube video.

One rant on Upworthy.

One Tweet.

One mis-step.

Today, "one" can be game changing.

But "one" can also be insignificant and disappear as fast as it emerged.

When that "one" presents itself, will you know how to respond?

## VALIDITY: CURRENCY OF THE HAWKS

# KNOW YOUR TRUTH

Urban Outfitters has squarely positioned itself as a brand obsessed with provocation, being a bold cultural informer. Merchandise is emotionally charged with politically incorrect t-shirts, edgy social games, and provocative coffee table books. Inspiring young adults to be bold and expressive, the brand constantly puts out products that ignite reaction, leaving the brand to consistently gauge their own line.

As a result, Urban Outfitters has found itself under countless attacks by offended watchdog groups and has to make regular decisions about what products are within brand boundaries and where they need to back off. Urban Outfitters' products have been the subject of multiple controversies, particularly concerning religious, ethical, and ethnic issues, including Ghettopoly, the "Everyone Loves a Jewish Girl" T-shirt designed with dollar signs, a controversial T-shirt saying "Eat Less" over the stomach, a T-shirt that featured a Palestinian child holding an AK-47 over the word "Victimized," sparkly handgun-shaped Christmas ornaments sold in city stores with high street crime, a set of Jesus Dress Up refrigerator magnets, St. Patrick's Day T-shirts portraying Irish people as drunks ... and the list goes on.

When a brand knows what it stands for, it can push its boundaries. And part of pushing boundaries means sometimes crossing them. A Free Range Brand is comfortable on the edge because it leads its pack. And when it goes too far, it can take a step back while still staying out front, rather than running to hide in the middle.

While Glade has spent millions trying to sell rancid smells as "ambiance," PooPourri hit nearly 29 million views on YouTube with foul honesty.

Direct and honest communication couched in blunt potty humor put PooPourri squarely into the Free Range arena—this brand is unapologetic. It knows its world, knows itself, and feels no shame. In less than a week, this brand went from unknown to over six million views.

Despite decades of consumer research, not one major air freshening brand has nailed relevancy in product, concept, targeting, usage occasion, packaging, messaging, and media choice like PooPourri. Shock value and humor aside, PooPourri understands the female consumer like these big brands don't and knows how to talk to them directly.

"Stand by your principles, and be comfortable with confrontation."

-Travis Kalanick, Uber CEO

## VALIDITY: CURRENCY OF THE HAWKS

## PRACTICE IT

Your platform must be part and parcel of everything you do, from internal culture to customer service. When it is not part of your bloodline, it doesn't matter how inspiring your message is—you risk achieving relevancy in the absence of authenticity, a potentially lethal position that will ultimately be exposed.

Look at Kmart. Outwitted by Target, Walmart, and Dollar stores, Kmart has never been able to find its footing ... until Draft FCB Chicago manufactured a believable, contemporary and resonant voice for the brand with "Ship My Pants" and "Big Gas Savings." The ads beautifully repositioned Kmart from a cheap discounter to a smart, value brand for a savvy, cost-conscious shopper. The ads instantly hit a sweet spot and reignited the brand to be once again considered by long-lost consumers. Is clever humor something the Kmart brand had been built upon? No. Can it claim it and own it? Absolutely. Does it deliver? Not a chance.

Authenticity can't be claimed on the surface—it needs to be practiced.

Anyone who walked into a Kmart store found the fun settled back to mothball dust. The in-store experience was nothing pleasant, unexpected, or uplifting as the ads suggested of the "new" Kmart experience. Stores were in poor physical shape, merchandising was in disarray, pricing was higher than competition, and the staff were

# BLOODLINE

# NOT

# TAGLINE

FREE RANGE BRANDS

unknowledgeable, unpleasant, and unavailable. Relevancy without authenticity. Poser.

Contrast that with Kimpton Hotels. The Hotel group has built its brand on the platform of Individuality. The brand actively embodies Individuality in the breadth of personalities, styles, and differences in employees, and then expresses that value by teaching the staff how to interact with guests on a very individualized level. They believe humor contributes to creativity, comfort, and individuality and call it "Kimpton Magic." Guests can feel it, and their experience makes them feel unique and special. They remember the feeling and look forward to experiencing it again, although the next time it may be a very different interpretation of the platform. Kimpton doesn't try to be everything to everyone and keeps its footprint small, but remains powerfully true to its bloodline.

Let's compare the authentic bloodline of Urban Outfitters with Zen Poser, Lululemon. On the surface, Lululemon gave yoga practicing women an alternative to hippie fashion while still embracing the principles of yoga, boasting an inspiring life manifesto printed on every red tote. But when CEO Chip Wilson, the ugly wizard behind the curtain, suggested that "some women" shouldn't wear Lululemon yoga pants, the crack exposed the soul of the company, and it was a disconnect from its outward persona.

"Does Lululemon want women to be comfortable in their clothing, or uncomfortable in our own bodies?" asked the Change.org petition. "Lululemon keeps shaming women's bodies--and this must stop."

From female shaman to shamer, fallout followed fast with attacks and accusation of Mr. Walker making racial slurs and degrading women, ultimately causing stock prices to take a downward dog and Chip Wilson to take a permanent savasana.

Taken out of context? Overly inflated? Unproven? Doesn't matter. What mattered was the snowballing hatred of the brand among its target: women. No diligence in the practice. Only posturing. Namaste!

Meanwhile, despite the list of complaints against Urban Outfitters, there is not a single mention of the brand on Change.org or any real traction of movements against the corporate brand. Why? Being provocative is core to Urban Outfitter's authenticity.

When "bloodline" and "tagline" reinforce each other, your brand is poised to be a powerful force.

## VALIDITY: CURRENCY OF THE HAWKS

## ADAPT. DON'T DEFEND.

If you're good enough to capture hearts and imaginations, prepare to be tested. Your authenticity must be validated to its core, or you'll be nothing more than another Poser.

While you have infinitely more ways to tell your story, your story can be easily exposed almost instantly. From leadership to ingredients, to sourcing, to internal culture, every piece of you will either validate or erode your credibility.

Gone are the days of company mis-steps or ugly baggage getting buried in the customer call center.

Today's brands are tested on a very public stage.

When it was LEGO's turn to stand trial as Greenpeace dragged the beloved brand into its battle with Shell to stop Arctic drilling, the brand had to make a choice: distance itself by side-stepping the Greenpeace/Shell debate or take a public stand.

The Greenpeace campaign using LEGO was jarring in that it clashed sweet childhood innocence with dark corporate ugliness. The widespread attention the campaign received, good and bad, was a slam-dunk for Greenpeace as it sparked a global dialogue with LEGO at the stake. So what was LEGO to do?

LEGO certainly wasn't a small or obscure Shell partner. The brands had a lucrative partnership, worth an estimated $116 million. At least 16 million Shell-branded LEGO sets had been sold in 26

never
hide
never
defend.

ADAPT

FREE RANGE
BRANDS

countries and LEGO also just released a series of LEGO Arctic building sets. There was no hiding there.

As their first response, LEGO decided to absolve themselves from the debate: LEGO Group CEO Jorgen Vig Knudstorp responded: "We firmly believe that this matter must be handled between Shell and Greenpeace. We are saddened when the LEGO brand is used as a tool in any dispute between organizations."

But it wasn't long before LEGO recognized the opportunity that existed for its brand while up on this stage. After all, the global LEGO brand has a corporate value of being committed to the environment.

LEGO has always proven itself to be a great Free Range Brand, reinventing itself, exploring new terrain, and flying on a higher emotional plane than a collection of functional toy offerings. But when Free Range Brands run into trouble, they don't run for cover. They take unexpected and unprecedented action. They reframe the conversation. They adapt.

And soon, in great Free Range form, LEGO severed its ties with Shell Oil, standing behind its conviction over short-term profits.

## VALIDITY: CURRENCY OF THE HAWKS

# HARNESS

Millennials and Boomers share a penchant for justice.

Team Mobile tapped into that need by coming out of the woodwork with a bold campaign built off the bottled-up collective anger towards AT&T's suffocating contracts and phone-upgrade deprivation. T-Mobile came riding in to end the tyrannical reign AT&T has had over its captive citizens.

Billing itself as the "Uncarrier," Team Mobile distanced itself from the bad behavior that stigmatized the industry. Not only did T-Mobile fight back, but the brand gave customers the opportunity to throw a well-deserved punch in the process (a smart Hacker move).

Bold, playful, and everything a Millennial would want, The Break-Up campaign couldn't make it easier or more enjoyable to give AT&T a straight-up smack in the face. Hawks could select how they wanted to deliver their punch and T-Mobile took care of the dirty work, picking up any fees along the way. Of course, they could then share their bold move with their friends, the Mobile Lords.

Team Mobile's campaign harnessed the Hawks' need for justice, Hackers' love of customization, and Lords' desire to discover and share. Collectively, they made customers into Lovers and gave AT&T a well-deserved kick in the ass.

## IGNITING VALIDITY

# HANDLE YOUR HAWKS

Hawks want to influence with purpose.

1. If you are successful and your voice is heard, it will be challenged. Are you clear on what you stand for? Is everyone in your organization?

2. When challenges come, are you prepared to stand by your truth? Is everyone in your organization?

3. What parts of your organization are not aligned with what you stand for? Consider leadership, product components, sourcing, internal culture, who you hire, how you treat employees, and how your organization is committed to the greater community. Again, it is not incumbent upon you to do more than you are capable of. It is incumbent upon you to be aligned to your truth.

4. When the unexpected happens, do your best to make it right. Connect personally, proactively, humbly, and repeatedly. Make tough choices.

# FREE RANGE CURRENCY

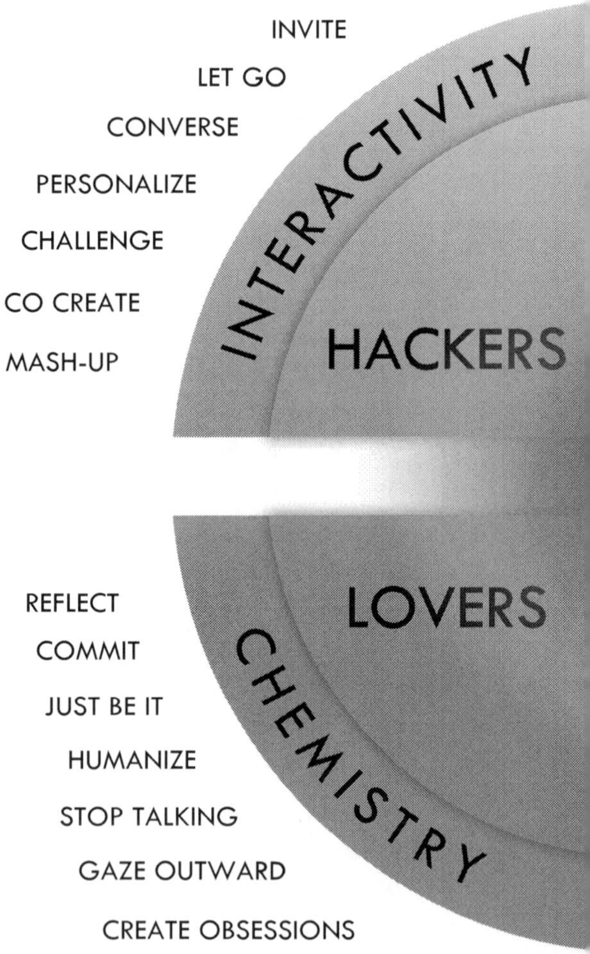

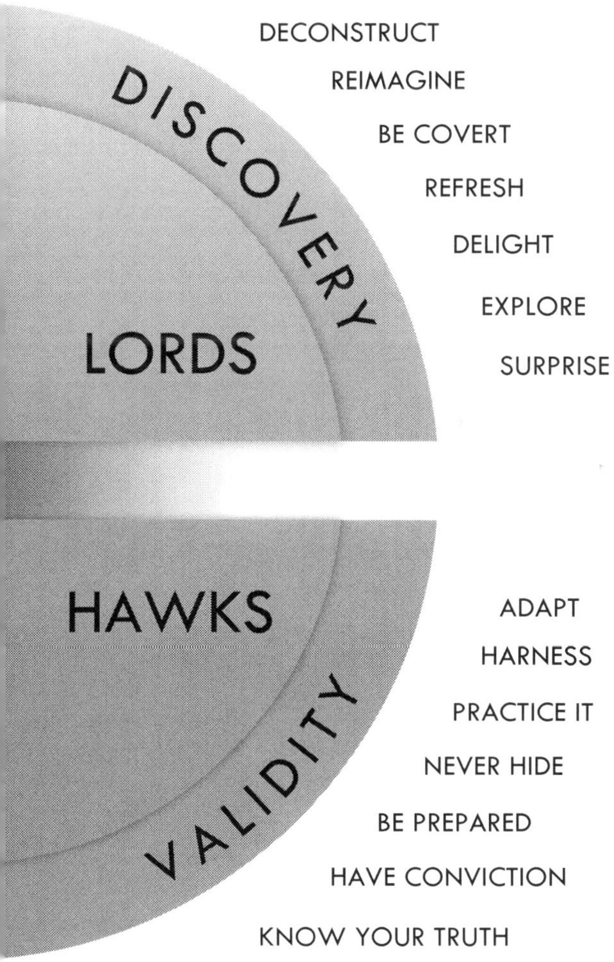
DECONSTRUCT
REIMAGINE
BE COVERT
REFRESH
DELIGHT
EXPLORE
SURPRISE
DISCOVERY
LORDS
HAWKS
VALIDITY
ADAPT
HARNESS
PRACTICE IT
NEVER HIDE
BE PREPARED
HAVE CONVICTION
KNOW YOUR TRUTH

# V

# FINAL QUESTION

# WHAT KIND OF BRAND ARE YOU BUILDING?

Free Range Brands have evolved from their broadcast-era ancestors when all messaging was led by the marketer. Free Range Brands know that today, true authenticity can only be manifested by the community, not peddled by the brand. So letting go, rather than controlling, becomes the key to modern brand building.

Free Range Brands position themselves to embrace this new reality by fixing their sights on goals that are beyond brand-centric; platforms that communities can participate in, perhaps even lead. A Free Range Brand leads by its soul, knows what it stands for, when to exert control, and when to let go.

It thrives in open waters and boldly rides the waves of unpredictability to explore uncharted paths. A Free Range Brand doesn't get lost reinventing itself to be relevant, first, loudest, or unexpected. It survives by determination and agility, enabling it to travel and explore without losing its way.

Both Free Range Brands and Tethered Brands may seem similar on the surface. Both can actively hire the most creative agencies to develop engaging and relevant creative. Both can develop campaigns that get talked about. Both can support philanthropic efforts to show they care.

Free Range Brands can be corporate, mainstream, and have mass appeal, like Heineken, Oreo, Taco Bell, and Urban Outfitters. Tethered Brands use that as an excuse.

DON'T
ON OLD HARDWARE
OPERATE
FREE RANGE
BRANDS

Free Range Brands explore and roam in ways Tethered Brands fear.

The difference isn't in what programs they launch. The difference is in the way they think, the way they learn, and the way they evolve.

So, what kind of brand are you creating?

*Adapt or Die*

73626121R00098

Made in the USA
Columbia, SC
15 July 2017